NEW TECHNOLOGY

military technology

Ian Graham

A⁺

Smart Apple Media

This book has been published in cooperation with Evans Publishing Group.

© Evans Brothers Limited 2008
This edition published under license from Evans Brothers Limited.

Published in the United States by Smart Apple Media, an imprint of Black Rabbit Books
P.O. Box 3263, Mankato, Minnesota 56002

Printed in the United States

Library of Congress Cataloging-in-Publication Data

Graham, Ian, 1953–
    Military technology / Ian Graham.
    p. cm.—(Smart Apple Media. New technology)
    Includes index.
    Summary: "Describes new technologies that are helping make military aviation, land warfare, warships and submarines, intelligence, non-lethal weapons, and space weapons more efficient and discusses the implications these technologies have on current and future warfare"—Provided by publisher.
    ISBN 978-1-59920-165-8
    1. United States—Armed Forces—Weapons systems—Juvenile literature. 2. Weapons systems—Juvenile literature. 3. Military art and science—Effect of technological innovations on—Juvenile literature. I. Title.
UF500.G74 2008
355'.070973—dc22
                                    2008000441

Credits

Series Editor: Paul Humphrey
Editor: Gianna Williams
Designer: Keith Williams
Production: Jenny Mulvanny
Picture researchers: Rachel Tisdale
    and Laura Embriaco
Consultant: Iain MacGregor, author and editor specialized in military history.

Acknowledgements

Title page: Northrop Grumman Integrated Systems; p.6 Msgt Thomas J. Menequin, USAF/Department of Defense; p.7 U.S. Air Force; p.9 Dennis Rogers/U.S. Air Force; p.10 Department of Defense; p.11 David Gossett, Teledyne Ryan Aeronautical/ Department of Defense; p.12 Northrop Grumman Integrated Systems; p.13 Boeing; p.14 R. D. Ward, CIV/Department of Defense; p.15 Berkeley Robotics and Human Engineering Laboratory; p.16 ©2007 Vecna Technologies, Inc.; p.17 Mass Communication Specialist 3rd Class Kenneth G. Takada/U.S. Navy; p.18 Master Sgt. Ken Hammond/Department of Defense; p.19 LCPL Sarah M. Harman, USMC/ Department of Defense; p.20 Naval Sea Systems Command/U.S. Navy; p.21 Kockums AB; p.22 General Dynamics/U.S. Navy; p.24 YN1 Ivan Rivera, USN/Department of Defense; p.25 top Photographer's Mate 2nd Class Lynn Friant/ U.S. Navy; p.25 Wikimedia Commons; p.26 Tech. Sgt. Shane A. Cuomo/U.S. Air Force; p.27 Tech. Sgt. Paul Dean/U.S. Air Force; p.28 R. Fearing/UC Berkeley; p.29 Lockheed Martin; p.31 Eamonn Bourke, Army.mil; p.32 Randy Montoya/Sandia National Laboratories; p.33 Airman 1st Class Gina Chiaverotti/Army.mil; pp.34-35 Courtesy of Taser International; p.37 American Technology Corporation; p.38 Reynolds/ Department of Defense; p.39 U.S. Department of Defense; p.40 U.S. Department of Defense/Science Photo Library; p.41 Michael Savell/Department of Defense; p.42 Ed Kashi/Corbis; p.43 Peter Macdiarmid/Getty Images.

contents

introduction

Military technology is enormously varied. It includes land, sea, and air vehicles of all sorts, communications and computer systems, weapons, satellites, and robots. This technology is constantly being updated as military forces try to stay one step ahead of each other.

How is new military technology developed? Military technology cannot stand still. Each time a new development provides a better means of attack, it has to be answered by a better means of defense. The best guns, tanks, fighter planes, warships, and missiles give one side an advantage in battle . . . until someone else develops even better versions of the same weapons. Military scientists and engineers are constantly looking for new ways of using materials, engines, and electronics to improve existing technology. Sometimes, military forces spot a need for a particular system, vehicle, or weapon, perhaps a new type of plane or warship. The government may ask manufacturers to come up with designs. Two or more of the ideas put forward may then be built and tested to find the best one.

Monitoring communications during a military exercise. Better, faster communications technology is crucial to military success.

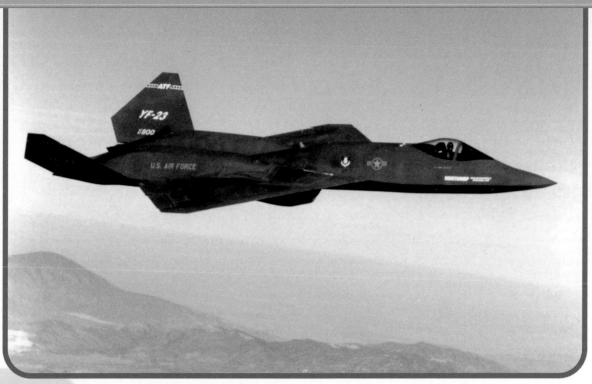

Not all new designs go on to be adopted by the armed forces. The United States (U.S.) Air Force decided not to develop the Northrop YF-23 prototype fighter (above).

The successful design will go on to be manufactured and issued to military forces.

Reaching further The range, or reach, of weapons has increased greatly. The first weapons made thousands of years ago were used in hand-to-hand fighting or as far as someone could throw them. Modern artillery can fire exploding shells more than 18 miles (30 km) and the most powerful rocket-propelled missiles can travel 5,000 miles (8,000 km).

What does it cost? As military technology has advanced, its cost has soared. A modern fighter plane costs about $300 million to develop and build. A modern bomber plane costs more than $2 billion. A Nimitz class nuclear-powered aircraft carrier costs about $4.4 billion.

Some countries spend a lot more money on military technology than others. The United States spends the most. Its military spending is nearly 10 times more than the next biggest spender, China. In fact, the U.S. spends more than the next 14 countries added together.

This book reveals the latest military equipment in service today and looks at the new military technology that is coming in the next few years.

CHAPTER 1
military aviation

Aviation is one of the most competitive areas of military technology. The leading military powers keep trying to outdo each other in the design of better, faster, and more maneuverable combat planes.

Why are fighters so important?

Military action often begins with an attack from the air to clear the sky of enemy aircraft and destroy enemy tanks, radar, missile launchers, and other threats on the ground. This is the job of the fighter. Winning the air war enables ground forces to move in more easily.

Stealth planes A whole new

generation of fighter planes is entering service. The first of these is the F-22 Raptor, made by Lockheed Martin and

A stealth plane's shape reflects radar waves away from the dish that sent them.

Boeing. Its engines are more advanced, its electronic systems are smarter, and it is a stealth plane. The B-2 Spirit bomber is a stealth plane, too. It served in the Kosovo War, the invasion of Afghanistan, and both Gulf wars.

HOW IT WORKS

A stealth plane is designed to be almost invisible to radar. Its shape reflects radar waves away from enemy radar instead of toward it. The plane can also be covered with special materials that soak up some of the radar waves instead of reflecting them.

Signal is reflected away from ground station

Radar signal from ground station

An Osprey tiltrotor hovers in the air. Its spinning rotors provide all the lift needed to support its weight. They enable it to take off and land without a runway.

Vertical takeoff Military forces use a variety of vertical takeoff aircraft. Nearly all of them are helicopters. There are small attack helicopters like the U.S. Apache and German Tiger, bigger medium-lift helicopters like the Black Hawk, and even bigger heavy-lift transport helicopters like the twin-rotor Chinook. Now there is a new type of vertical takeoff aircraft called a "tiltrotor." It has rotors like a helicopter and wings like a plane. To take off, its propellers work like helicopter rotors. They lift it straight up in the air. After takeoff, its engines and propellers tilt forward, and it flies like a normal plane.

A fighter of the future – the F-35

The F-35 Lightning II is a future fighter being developed now. The U.S. Air Force, U.S. Navy, and U.S. Marines will all fly the F-35. These three military services need different types of aircraft, so three different F-35s will be built. The F-35 flown by the Marines, for example, will be able to land vertically. The F-35 flown by the Navy will be designed specially for use on aircraft carriers. More than three-fourths of their parts will be the same, so building the planes and repairing them will be easier, faster, and less expensive. Like the F-22, the F-35 will be a stealth

WHAT'S NEXT?

Hypersonic combat planes are planes that can fly faster than five times the speed of sound. Hypersonic planes could fly to anywhere in the world within a few hours. The U.S. Air Force plans to have a manned hypersonic fighter flying by about 2025.

Planes without pilots It is possible for a pilot to fly a plane without actually being in the plane! The plane is flown by remote control from the ground. Planes like this are called UAVs (Unmanned Air Vehicles) or RPVs (Remotely Piloted Vehicles). These planes are mainly used to gather information about the enemy. The 49-foot (15-m) long Predator spy plane is a UAV. Predator has been in service with the U.S. Air Force since 1995. It has been used in the Balkans, Afghanistan, Yemen, and Iraq. It has also been used by the Italian Air Force since 2004 and the RAF since 2006.

The most advanced UAVs do not even need a pilot on the ground. They are programmed with a mission, and

plane. The first F-35s should begin entering service in about 2011. In addition to the U.S. military, the British Royal Air Force (RAF) and Royal Navy, as well as the Italian Navy, will also fly them.

The Lockheed Martin F-35 Lightning II future fighter is being developed from its X-35 experimental aircraft. The F-35 is expected to cost $40 billion to develop.

The Global Hawk unmanned spy plane can survey, in one day, an area equivalent to the country of Greece.

HOW IT WORKS

The pilot of an unmanned air vehicle sits in a cockpit on the ground. The pilot looks at screens showing live images from cameras in the plane. When the pilot moves the controls, radio signals are sent to the plane to steer it.

fly from takeoff to landing under the control of their own computers.

Unmanned fighters The next generation of unmanned military aircraft will be fighters. Unmanned fighters are called UCAVs (Unmanned Combat Air Vehicles). They are already being built and flight tested by manufacturers in France and the U.S.

FOR AND AGAINST

For

- UCAVs are smaller and more maneuverable than manned fighters.
- They can go into action without risking the lives of pilots.
- They can deal with the most heavily defended targets in the early days of a war, to make the sky safer for the manned fighters that will follow them.

Against

- As pilots are not in danger, there may be a greater temptation to go to war.
- If a UCAV developed a fault, it could attack friendly forces or civilians by mistake.

UCAVs are faster and more maneuverable than UAVs. They are expected to start service some time after 2010.

Laser planes A laser is a device that produces an intense beam of pure light. Lasers are used in DVD players and communications. There are military lasers, too, but until now they have been used mostly in weapons-guidance systems, not as weapons.

Below is a computer-generated image of a UCAV destroying a target. This UCAV is being developed by the Joint Unmanned Combat Air Systems (J-UCAS) project. Experimental planes have already been built and flown.

The ABL airborne laser missile system aims a laser at its target from the nose of the aircraft, which can rotate.

HOW IT WORKS

When a high-power laser is fired from an aircraft, it produces intense heat in the target. This weakens the target or even cuts through it. It could make a plane or a missile break up in the air or make its fuel explode.

A laser gunsight sends out a thin beam of light for aiming a gun. Tank gunners use laser range-finders to measure the distance to a target. Lasers are also used in devices called target designators. They fire a laser beam at a target such as a building. A laser-guided bomb steers itself toward the laser reflection and hits the target. Now, super powerful lasers are being developed as weapons for military aircraft. The aircraft company Boeing will soon begin tests of laser planes.

WHAT'S NEXT?

An aircraft laser being developed now is so powerful that it will be able to destroy a target 9.3 miles (15 km) away. The planes that will have this laser, the Boeing 747 freighter and the C-130 Hercules aircraft, have already made test flights, and the high-power laser weapon has been tested on the ground.

CHAPTER 2
land warfare

Land warfare depends on soldiers, and soldiers depend on their weapons, vehicles, protective clothing, and equipment. In the next 20 years, these will be transformed, making future soldiers better protected, better armed, better informed, and more comfortable.

Military clothing In the past, a uniform simply identified a soldier's fighting force and rank. Today, the high-tech-materials combat clothing is made to protect soldiers from all sorts of weather. There is also special-purpose clothing made of materials that give extra protection from fire or from nuclear, biological, or chemical attacks. New military clothing in development does a lot more than this. Borrowing a system already used in spacesuits, a new layer next to the skin will have liquid circulating through it to keep the soldier at a comfortable temperature, however hot or cold the weather. The uniform may also have sensors embedded in it to monitor the soldier's heart rate, temperature, and other factors. Problems with the soldier's health

The U.S. Army's prototype combat uniform is presented at a press briefing at the Pentagon, headquarters of the U.S. Department of Defense. The helmet is fitted with video cameras and satellite navigation. The uniform is armored and can be heated or cooled.

will be relayed to commanders, and if a soldier is wounded, the system will give vital information to medics.

Armored uniforms As well as a helmet, soldiers can wear a flak jacket designed to stop bullets and flying debris from explosions. They often also wear body armor for extra protection. This is made of hard plates that fit inside pockets in a special vest. Future soldiers will wear clothing that stays flexible until a bullet hits it, when it instantly hardens like an armor plate. It sounds like science fiction, but it already exists, and two different versions have been developed by companies in the U.S. It is based on new materials made of super-strong fibers that lock together only when they are hit hard.

Military robots Robot vehicles already help with bomb disposal and reconnaissance. Some are small enough and light enough to be carried on a soldier's back. The payloads they can carry include cameras and mechanical pincers.

Some of the remote-control robots

This soldier is wearing a prototype lower extremity exoskeleton. The powered leg braces enable a soldier to carry heavy loads more easily. The exoskeleton supports the weight of the backpack.

WHAT'S NEXT?

Future soldiers will be able to wear robot-like limbs called exoskeletons. An exoskeleton enables a soldier to move faster or carry heavier loads. One exoskeleton already tested enabled soldiers to lift a 240 lb (110 kg) load as if it weighed only 10 lb (4.5 kg). Another one enabled its wearer to move twice as fast as normal.

A Battlefield Extraction-Assist Robot (BEAR) demonstrates how it can pick up a wounded soldier. When it finds a casualty, it slides its arms underneath.

in use today have already been fitted with guns. A camera on the robot lets a soldier aim and fire the weapon from up to .6 mile (1 km) away. These armed robots are about to go into military service. Armed robot sentries have also been developed for guarding a country's borders.

One of the most dangerous jobs during a battle is the rescue of wounded soldiers. A robot called the Battlefield Extraction-Assist Robot (BEAR) has been designed to find and rescue wounded soldiers. A prototype has already been built.

Military vehicles Military vehicles range from small transport vehicles like the versatile Hummer to bigger and more powerful armored fighting vehicles. The most heavily armored military vehicles are tanks. Tank armor used to be made of thick metal, but modern tank armor is made of top-secret, multilayered plates of metal, ceramic, and plastic. Some tank armor

WHAT'S NEXT?

Military planners think robots will become increasingly like humans and able to act on their own. They will have enough artificial intelligence to find their own way around, identify enemy forces, and decide what to do.

A Talon military robot searches for a terrorist bomb, while a small spy craft called a Micro Air Vehicle (MAV) hovers overhead. Pictures from the MAV are used to guide the robot to the most promising areas.

Nuclear weapons Weapons of all sorts are used in warfare, from pistols and rifles for close combat, to mortars and tanks for short-range action, and artillery for long-range attack. There are also missiles ranging from small, short-range weapons fired from a soldier's shoulder to long-range missiles that can span an ocean.

Nuclear weapons are the most powerful of all. They are also known as "weapons of mass destruction" (WMD), because they can kill very large numbers

is even designed to explode when a missile hits it, to stop the missile from bursting through it. Tanks can weigh up to 77 tons (70 t). The tracks around their wheels spread their weight over a large area and stop them from getting bogged down in soft ground.

HOW IT WORKS

There are two main types of nuclear weapon—the atom bomb and the hydrogen bomb. An atom bomb works by breaking big atoms of uranium or plutonium apart. Each time an atom splits, it gives out a burst of energy. Millions of these add together to make a huge explosion. A hydrogen bomb produces an even more powerful explosion by slamming very light atoms together.

of people. One nuclear weapon may be as powerful as several million tons of ordinary explosives. There have been many tests of nuclear weapons, but only two have ever been used in war. They were atom bombs dropped on the Japanese cities of Hiroshima and Nagasaki at the end of World War II.

Nuclear proliferation Since the first nuclear weapons were developed, a growing number of countries have acquired them. As each country "goes nuclear," its possible enemies race to produce their own nuclear weapons. In time, most developed countries may have nuclear weapons. This may not make a full-scale nuclear war more likely, because any country that carries out a nuclear attack on another nuclear state knows that it risks suffering a devastating nuclear counterattack. This is called "Mutually Assured Destruction" (MAD). It has

prevented nuclear war until now. However, as the number of nuclear-armed states grows, there is more chance of a nuclear weapon being used by accident or falling into the hands of terrorists.

WHAT'S NEXT?

Small nuclear artillery shells and bombs could be used in the future as "bunker-busters" to destroy heavily strengthened underground buildings. A bunker-buster is designed to penetrate earth, rock, or concrete before its warhead explodes, instead of exploding in the air or on the surface. They have a very strong casing that can survive smashing into the ground. One version of the American B-61 nuclear bomb is a nuclear bunker-buster. It is designed to detonate 4 ft (1.2 m) underground and produce a shock wave powerful enough to crush a bunker below it.

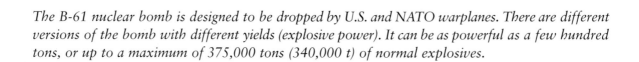

The B-61 nuclear bomb is designed to be dropped by U.S. and NATO warplanes. There are different versions of the bomb with different yields (explosive power). It can be as powerful as a few hundred tons, or up to a maximum of 375,000 tons (340,000 t) of normal explosives.

Dirty bombs A nuclear weapon doesn't have to produce a nuclear explosion to be effective. Simpler weapons called "dirty bombs" spread radioactive material over a wide area instead of producing a nuclear blast. A dirty bomb could make a modern city uninhabitable for decades. Dirty bombs have already been used. A dirty bomb was planted in Moscow by Chechen rebels in 1995, but it didn't explode. It was found and defused. Along with dynamite, it contained radioactive Caesium-137 taken from cancer treatment equipment. In London in 2006, Dhiren Barot was convicted of planning "dirty bomb" attacks in the United Kingdom (UK) and U.S.

Military staff check for radioactive contamination from a simulated "dirty bomb" attack during an exercise. Their suits protect them from radioactive particles falling

FOR AND AGAINST

For

- Nuclear weapons deter countries from attacking a nuclear state, because they risk a nuclear counterattack.

Against

- Nuclear weapons are incredibly expensive.
- As more countries acquire them, there is a greater risk of a nuclear accident.
- They are useless against terrorist organizations.
- They are indiscriminate. They can kill hundreds of thousands of people at a time.
- The radioactive fallout from a nuclear explosion damages the environment and people's health for decades and over a wide area.

CHAPTER 3
warships and submarines

Nations have used warships to spread their power overseas and control sea routes for centuries. Modern warships are big, slow targets that are very easy to find and attack. Future warships will be faster and harder to find. Under the waves, faster submarines armed with faster weapons are being developed, too.

Sea giants The biggest and most powerful warships ever built are the U.S. Navy's Nimitz-class aircraft carriers. Each of these giant ships is 1,092 ft (317 m) long, weighs 116,000 tons (100,000 t), and carries up to 90 aircraft. The ship and its aircraft need a total crew of nearly 6,000. Nuclear-powered engines give it a top speed of more than 35 mph (55 kph). Nimitz-class carriers served as floating military airports during both Gulf wars.

Stealth warships An enemy cannot attack a ship it cannot find. Warships are normally found by radar, so they need to have a shape that makes it hard for radar to spot them, just like stealth planes. The shape of a stealth warship stops enemy radar waves from being reflected back where they came from, so the ship disappears from radar screens.

The U.S. Navy's Sea Shadow stealth warship was the first stealth warship to be designed. It floats on two hulls, hidden under the water.

The U.S. Navy experimented with a stealth ship called *Sea Shadow* in the 1980s. The first stealth ship to enter service with a Navy was the Swedish Navy's *Visby*, launched in 2000. *Visby* is also the biggest ship to be built from carbon fiber, a super-strong plastic material used to make racing cars. Norway, France, Germany, Britain, India, and Singapore have stealth warships, too. The U.S. Navy's next stealth ship is the DD(X). It produces an echo, or blip, on a radar screen 50 times smaller than other warships. The first DD(X) ship, the USS *Zumwalt*, is due to enter service in about 2013.

The Swedish Navy's Visby *is a stealth ship. Its sloping sides reflect radio waves away from their source. This and a plastic hull make the ship almost undetectable by radar.*

Naval guns In the past, battleships were armed with mighty guns. A World War II battleship could hurl a shell weighing 2,700 lb (1,225 kg) a distance of more than 20 miles (32 km). Modern warships are armed with missiles. A Harpoon ship-to-ship missile has a range of 75 miles (140 km). Future warships may be armed with guns once more, but they will be a completely new type of gun called a "railgun." A railgun fires a projectile so fast that it can reach

The Littoral Combat Ship (LCS) is a new warship being developed for the U.S. Navy. It is a high-speed trimaran (three hulls) designed to operate in shallow coastal waters. A flight deck at the back serves as a landing platform for helicopters.

WHAT'S NEXT?

Some future warships may have three hulls instead of one. Ships with three hulls are called trimarans. Trimaran racing yachts and powerboats are common, but now trimarans are being designed as warships. They are very stable and fast, and they can operate in rough seas.

Power generator · Projectile · Conducting rails

Armature · Direction of flight

Pulsed power supply

A railgun uses a massive electric current to launch a projectile from between a pair of rails.

the horizon in only six seconds. It can also fire a projectile so high that it goes into space, and then uses satellite navigation to aim itself at a target before it falls back to Earth. Experimental railguns have already been built in the UK and the U.S. The first railgun-armed warship could be in service by 2020.

Submarines All the major military powers have submarines. They dive by letting seawater flood into tanks inside them, so that they become heavier than the surrounding water. Modern submarines can dive to a depth of 750–1,000 ft (240–300 m). At this depth, the sea squeezes a submarine's

HOW IT WORKS

A railgun has two parallel conducting rails with a block of metal, called the armature, between them. The armature slides along the rails. A huge electric current is sent down one rail, across the armature, and back up the other rail. This produces a powerful magnetic field, which makes the armature accelerate down the rails. A railgun projectile is a lump of metal, like a rifle bullet, only bigger. It's not like an artillery shell or guided missile—it has no explosives inside it. It travels so fast that it hits its target with as much energy as a conventional exploding shell. The projectile sits on the front of the armature, or inside it, and is shot from the end of the rails.

A railgun does not need the explosive charges that usually launch shells from guns. The projectile itself does not even need an explosive warhead. It hits a target so fast that it does not need to explode to destroy it. So, warships armed with railguns do not need to carry lots of highly explosive shells and charges. A naval railgun could replace the "million-dollars-a-shot" missiles that are used today, but at a fraction of the cost.

Naval officers man their battle stations onboard the U.S. Navy submarine Charlotte. *The* USS Charlotte *is a nuclear-powered attack submarine.*

WHAT'S NEXT?

Some people think it might be possible to build a supersonic submarine! The U.S. Navy tested a supersonic underwater weapon in 1997, so it is certainly possible for something to travel at supersonic speeds underwater.

hull 25-30 times more powerfully than at the surface. If it dives too deep, water pressure will crush it.

There are different types of submarines. Attack submarines hunt and attack enemy submarines and surface ships. Bigger ballistic-missile submarines patrol the oceans, staying hidden deep underwater. Their nuclear-powered engines enable them to stay underwater for several months. They make their own water and oxygen. The only reason they have to come to the surface is to fill their food stores. They carry a deadly cargo of nuclear weapons, but they do not attack other vessels. In fact, they avoid all other ships. Their job is to deter anyone from making a nuclear attack on their country. If this were to happen, these submarines could unleash a terrible counterattack.

The USS Florida *powers through the water. The* Florida *is one of the U.S. Navy's nuclear-powered Ohio-class guided missile submarines.* Florida *is armed with cruise missiles.*

Underwater rockets The torpedo is the submarine's standard weapon. Once launched into the water, it hones in on the sound of its target. When a vessel is attacked by torpedoes, its crew has a short time to take defensive action. A faster underwater weapon would give the target no time to react. Russia has developed just such a weapon, an underwater missile called Shkval. It is about four times faster than a normal torpedo.

HOW IT WORKS

The Shkval is fired from a submarine's torpedo tube. It has a rocket that propels it through the water at 220 mph (360 kph). It travels inside a coating of air bubbles that stream out of its nose. The bubbles stop the water from slowing it down.

A close-up of the Shkval underwater rocket shows clearly the hole at the tip of its nose where air streams out.

CHAPTER 4
intelligence

During a war, it is vital to know where enemy forces are, how strong they are, what they are doing, and what they are planning to do. This work is done by robot planes, wireless sensors, and satellites in space.

How is intelligence gathered?

Satellites and spy planes take photographs and listen to radio communications. Spy planes of the past, such as the Lockheed U-2 and SR-71 Blackbird, were manned aircraft. Manned spy planes were the best way of gathering intelligence for many years, but there are other ways of gathering intelligence today.

Micro spies

Many of the aircraft that do this work today have no pilot on board. They are either flown remotely by a pilot on the ground, or they are autonomous aircraft that fly themselves.

An airman views images from a Predator unmanned spy plane during a training mission. The plane is being flown by a pilot on the ground. The pictures it takes can be sent to screens anywhere in the world.

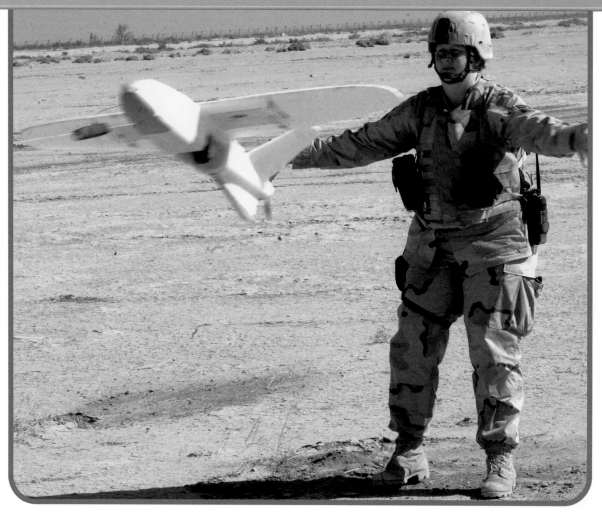

Predator is an unmanned spy plane with a wingspan of nearly 50 feet (15 m). The Global Hawk autonomous spy plane is twice as big. Smaller spy planes the size of a laptop computer, and even smaller insect-like spy planes, are being developed. They are small enough to be carried by a soldier and launched by hand. These tiny spy craft are called Micro Air Vehicles (MAVs).

Micro Air Vehicles One example of an MAV is called the Wasp. It is a tiny plane with a wingspan of just 12 inches (33

An airman launches an MAV in Iraq. The tiny spy plane is catapulted into the air and flies away.

cm). The whole plane with all of its onboard equipment weighs less than 1 lb (0.5 kg). It looks like a toy, but it is a serious spy plane. It has battery-powered video cameras at the front and back that transmit live pictures to its operator. Despite their tiny size, some MAVs also have their own miniature autopilot and satellite guidance.

MAVs have already been tested as a way of checking ships that the Navy

An artist's impression of what Lockheed's high-altitude airship will look like.

WHAT'S NEXT?

Unmanned, high-altitude airships will be able to circle over a trouble spot for days or weeks, relaying pictures by satellite to their base. These airships are filled with helium, a gas which is lighter than air. Lockheed is developing a high-altitude airship that will monitor a 600-mi (1,000-km) wide area of the ground from 12 mi (20 km) up. It will be nearly 500 ft (152 m) long and up to 150 ft (45 m) in diameter.

may want to board and search. Soldiers can also use them to check out an area before they advance into it. A soldier launches an MAV by starting its engine and throwing it into the air. The operator then steers the plane to the area of interest. Its cameras send pictures to a screen on a small, handheld unit. A MAV is so light that an operator can catch it on its return like a Frisbee.

Robofly could be considered an extreme example of an MAV. Robofly is a flying robot being developed at the University of California, Berkeley. It is called Robofly because it is a robot aircraft that is actually the size of a fly. One day, squads of roboflies could be sent out to search for targets and collect information about them.

Spy satellites Military satellites orbit the Earth carrying cameras that can see objects on the ground below as small as only 1.5 in (4 cm) across. Some of them have infrared cameras that see heat instead of light, so they work in the dark. They also listen to radio communications. Details of spy satellites are top secret, but the latest spy satellites are thought to use stealth technology to make them difficult to find and attack. In the future, they may use lasers instead of radio to send information to Earth. Laser communications are more difficult for an enemy to intercept than radio. When a spacecraft runs out of fuel for its engines, it cannot maneuver anymore and its working life is over. The latest spy satellites may be capable of being refueled by automatic space tankers, enabling them to stay in space for longer and maneuver from place to place more easily.

Electronic warfare Modern warfare relies so heavily on radar, computers, communications, and other electronic equipment that a lot of work goes into finding ways to attack enemy electronic systems and protect friendly systems. This is electronic warfare.

How are electronic systems attacked? One way to attack enemy radar and communications is to transmit radio signals that jam them. Electronic-warfare aircraft are packed with listening equipment and jamming equipment. As they circle over an area, they pick up enemy radio signals, analyze them, and transmit radio signals to jam them. Alternatively, electronic equipment can be knocked out by a new type of weapon called an

HOW IT WORKS

The way EMPs work is top-secret. They may work by using a high-voltage coil to produce a strong magnetic field. Then an explosive is set off inside the coil. As the explosion moves through the coil, from one end to the other, it compresses the magnetic field ahead of it and strengthens it enormously, sending out a huge electromagnetic pulse, or EMP. When an EMP from an E-bomb hits radio antennas and electronic equipment, it makes large electric currents flow through them, burning out the electronics.

Atom in the air

Electron emits EMP

Gamma ray from nuclear explosion

"electronic bomb," or "E-bomb." It produces a powerful burst of energy called an electromagnetic pulse (EMP), which destroys electronic equipment. Any equipment can be protected from EMP by enclosing it in a metal box or cage called a Faraday cage. The simplest Faraday cage could be a cardboard box covered with metal foil. The military version is a custom-built metal container. However, antennas, controls, indicators, and sensors have to be outside the cage, so the EMP may still be able to destroy the equipment.

Scientists discovered the effects of EMPs when nuclear weapons were being tested in the 1950s, because nuclear explosions produce them. In 1962, a hydrogen bomb test over Johnston Island in the Pacific Ocean produced an EMP powerful enough to blow out 300 street lights 1,000 miles (1,600 km) away in Hawaii.

Robot spies One alternative to photographing the ground from the air or from space is to put devices on the ground to spy on military activities. These devices are called Unattended Ground Sensors (UGS). There are lots

Gamma rays from a nuclear explosion knock electrons out of atoms in the air. These electrons fly away through the Earth's magnetic field and give out a burst of energy called an EMP.

of different types. In addition to cameras, there are microphones, geophones (vibration detectors), magnetometers, heat sensors, and thermal (heat) imagers. The most advanced microphones analyze the sounds they pick up and only raise an alarm when they identify a particular type of sound—from passing tanks, for example. The latest sensors can link up with each other and work together. One sensor monitors the nearby area every few seconds, while other nearby

The aerials on top of these unattended ground sensors send information back to base by radio. Sensors may be camouflaged so they are harder for the enemy to spot. Their batteries keep them working for several weeks or more.

sensors stay in a "sleeping" or standby mode. When it detects something of interest, it "wakes up" the other sensors to take digital photographs and gather other types of information.

Seabed sensors During the Cold War, the U.S. wanted to know when Soviet submarines sailed into the Atlantic Ocean. They put a network of sensors on the seabed near Greenland, Iceland, and the UK. It was called "SOSUS (SOund SUrveillance System)." It picked up the sound of passing submarines. SOSUS is still used today, but only for scientific research.

WHAT'S NEXT?

The next generation of ground sensors will be smaller than ever and used in greater numbers than ever. They are called "Massively Deployed Unattended Ground Sensors (MDUGS)." They are smart enough to communicate with each other and form a map of enemy activity in an area. Two companies are known to be working on MDUGS. There were demonstrations of the systems in 2006. Field tests are going on now, and systems could be operational by 2011.

CHAPTER 5
nonlethal weapons

Nonlethal weapons are devices that stop enemy troops from advancing or move them out of an area without doing them any serious or lasting harm. They can also be used against rioters and aircraft hijackers.

Nonlethal weapons already in use today include tear gas, water cannons, and plastic bullets. The latest nonlethal weapons use dazzling lasers, heat rays, electric shocks, and very loud sounds. They are all designed to surprise people or put them out of action in a safe way.

Heat rays Heat rays have been a dream of inventors for centuries. Now there is one that really works. It's called the Active Denial System (ADS). When it is aimed at troops or rioters, it makes them feel as if their skin is burning. It can be mounted on a building that needs protection, but it is also small enough to be carried by a vehicle. This mobile version is called the Vehicle-Mounted Active Denial System (V-MADS). It can be used against people up to about 2,500 feet (750 m) away. The V-MADS is being

Researchers at the Sandia National Laboratories in New Mexico fine-tune a small-sized ADS. The small-sized ADS is being developed from the larger military unit. It will be used to protect buildings such as nuclear power stations.

HOW IT WORKS

V-MADS works like an amazingly powerful microwave oven. It sends out a narrow beam of microwaves (very short radio waves). When they hit someone, they travel through the skin. They make water molecules in the skin vibrate and heat up. This activates pain sensors in the skin. A 2-second burst of the waves can heat skin to 120°F (50°C). The pain makes people move away fast, but does no lasting damage.

developed for U.S. military forces. A fully developed system was demonstrated in 2007. It is likely to enter service with U.S. forces in 2010.

Electric-shock weapons Electric-shock weapons deliver electric shocks to a person's body. The electric-shock weapons used today include stun guns and tasers. A stun gun gives

The U.S. Army is testing the V-MADS. The antenna on top of the vehicle sends out a beam of energy that people feel as heat.

HOW IT WORKS

The human body controls its muscles by electric signals that travel along nerves from the brain. The body's electrical impulses are tiny, just a fraction of a volt. An electric shock weapon floods the body with between 20,000 and 150,000 volts. It overwhelms the body's own electrical system, which shuts down, and muscle control is lost for a while.

someone an electric shock when it is pushed against them and switched on. Tasers fire darts that deliver powerful electric shocks when they hit someone. The electric charge is carried by fine wires that connect the taser to the darts.

More advanced electric-shock weapons are being developed. These include electric bullets. They deliver an electric shock to anyone they hit. They can be fired by standard shotguns and grenade launchers. Electric bullets are in the final stage of development.

A taser gun

A taser fires small metal probes at a target up to 21 feet (6.4 m) away. Hooks anchor the probes in skin or clothing. Then a high-voltage charge travels along wires from the gun to the probes.

WHAT'S NEXT?

The next electric-shock weapons will use lasers instead of wires to deliver an electric shock. A laser beam aimed at the target will form a channel through the air that conducts electricity. A fraction of a second later, the high-voltage charge will be sent along this invisible conducting channel, like a lightning flash during a storm. Weapons like this are called "electrolasers" and are currently in development.

Acoustic weapons Acoustic weapons produce very loud sound. Troops often use "flash-bang" charges or flash grenades to surprise enemy forces with a sudden, unexpected explosion. Now, more advanced acoustic weapons are being developed.

The "vortex ring gun" fires a blank cartridge into a specially shaped barrel that sends out a doughnut-shaped pulse of air. In tests, it was able to knock down a full-size human dummy from 30 ft (10 m) away. Another weapon called the "stick radiator" is all electric. It's a tube about 3 feet (1 m) long and 1.5 in (4 cm) across. An electrical signal

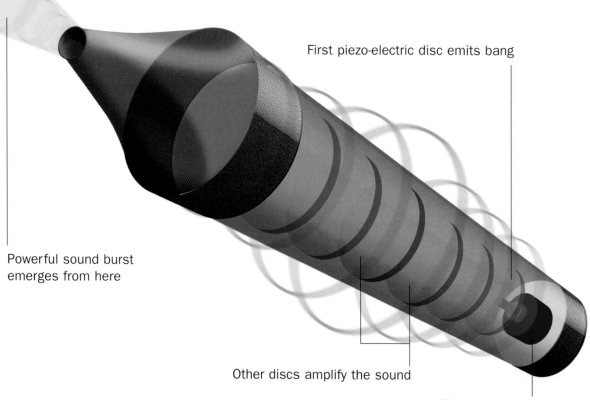

First piezo-electric disc emits bang

Powerful sound burst
emerges from here

Other discs amplify the sound

Electrical signal
emitted from here

A stick radiator fires bursts of sound created by piezo-electric discs that fire in sequence.

HOW IT WORKS

Acoustic weapons can work in two ways. First, they can produce sound so loud that it is painful to hear. This makes it very difficult for troops to fight at their best. Second, the "boom" produced by an acoustic weapon can be so powerful that the shock wave traveling through the air may actually knock someone over.

makes a device called a "piezo-electric disc" send a bang along the tube. This bang is not an explosion but a loud noise and a burst of energy. It reaches a second disc, which produces another bang at exactly the right moment to magnify the first bang. A series of these discs keeps magnifying the sound as it travels down the tube. The result is a painfully loud pulse of sound that travels through the air like a shock wave, and punches someone like a sound bullet.

Another new weapon called a "Pulsed Energy Projectile" (PEP) works in a different way. It uses a laser to produce a bright, hot flash. This heats the air so fast, like a bolt of lightning, that it produces a shock wave which travels through the air. It can knock over anyone it hits.

In 2005, pirates attacked a passenger liner off the coast of Somalia. The ship was equipped with the "Long Range Acoustic Device" (LRAD). The LRAD was designed to send out spoken messages over a distance of up to 3,300 feet (1,000 m), like a very loud megaphone, but it can also be used as a weapon. The liner's crew used it to aim loud bangs at the pirates, as if they were under attack. It stopped them from boarding the ship long enough for it to build up speed and outrun the pirate boats.

An operator with an LRAD. An LRAD machine can be used simply to communicate with distant ships as well as deter an actual attack, as happened in Somalia in 2005.

CHAPTER 6
space weapons

Satellites are so important for communications, gathering intelligence, navigation, and guiding weapons that they are likely to be attacked in a future war. Weapons may even be stationed in orbit to attack satellites, missiles in flight, and targets on the ground.

Satellites under attack Satellites in orbit are in a good position to spot enemy missiles climbing away from their launch pads. They can then sound an early warning of an attack. In a future war, these satellites could be destroyed just before intercontinental missiles are launched. These satellites would probably be attacked with antisatellite (ASAT) missiles. These missiles have already been developed and tested.

The first ASAT missiles were tested in the 1960s. They were not very accurate, and they usually missed their targets. There was a suggestion that nuclear weapons might be used instead.

Their blasts would be so powerful that they would not have to actually hit satellites to destroy them. However, they would also have spread deadly radioactive fallout around the Earth, and if shot down, their nuclear warheads could have landed anywhere. The Outer Space Treaty of 1967 banned the use of nuclear weapons in space. Missiles continued to improve, and by the 1980s, they had become accurate enough to hit satellites.

This F-15 fighter is carrying an ASAT missile underneath it. Flight tests with ASAT missiles began in 1982. Testing led to the successful destruction of a satellite in space by an air-launched ASAT missile in 1985.

Who has antisatellite missiles?

The U.S. and the Soviet Union both tested ASAT missiles until the 1980s. They had to end their tests because of the danger to orbiting satellites from wreckage sent flying in all directions by exploding missiles. Some of the debris from these tests still orbits the Earth today. Then on January 11, 2007, China successfully tested an ASAT missile by shooting down one of its own old weather satellites.

An ASAT missile soars away from an F-15 fighter. The aircraft pulls up into a steep climb before firing the missile. The missile then climbs into space and hones in on its target.

FOR AND AGAINST

For
- Weapons in space could attack targets anywhere on Earth without having to fly through other countries' airspaces.
- They could also attack satellites in space.

Against
- They would spark a new arms race in space.
- Exploding weapons and satellites in space would spread dangerous debris around the Earth.

Antisatellite satellites

"Antisatellite satellites" could be used instead of missiles to attack enemy satellites. They work by maneuvering close to an enemy satellite and exploding. Another way to knock out satellites without blowing them up is to blind their cameras by firing lasers at them from the ground or from an aircraft. This has the advantage of disabling satellites without producing any debris or wreckage in space.

Other space weapons One space weapon being researched now does not use any explosives or lasers. It is a satellite armed with large tungsten rods. Each of the metal rods is about 20 ft (6 m) long and 12 in (30 cm) across. They would be fired at a target on Earth, hitting it without warning at more than 8,000 mph (13,000 kph). The speed and weight of the rod would make it amazingly destructive. It could penetrate buildings, tanks, and even underground bunkers.

"STAR WARS"

"Star Wars" is the nickname of a U.S. project called the "Strategic Defense Initiative (SDI)" in the 1980s. The project was to use weapons on the ground and in space to protect the U.S. from missile attacks. The system was to include laser weapons in space, but they proved to be impractical. However, the different parts of the SDI system—such as missiles, lasers, railguns, weapons in space, and sensors—are still being developed.

A Titan 1 missile is destroyed by a laser in a test at the White Sands Missile Range in New Mexico. The experiment was carried out to test the effectiveness of laser weapons as part of the Star Wars project.

Technicians work on the Low-power Atmospheric Compensation Experiment (LACE) satellite. This satellite was an important part of developing laser weapons for the SDI or Star Wars project.

Will there be manned military spacecraft?

There are manned military vehicles on land and water, underwater, and in the air. In the future, there will very likely be manned military spacecraft, too. There have already been military space stations. Three of Russia's seven *Salyut* space stations in the 1970s were military. They were mainly used for photo-reconnaissance, taking highly detailed photographs of certain parts of the Earth. One of them, *Salyut 3*, was even armed with a gun. After its crew left, the gun was successfully test fired in space. The U.S. space shuttle has carried out military space missions, too. In the future, there are likely to be more manned military spacecraft flown by military astronauts.

conclusion

Military powers used to compete with each other to arm themselves with the most powerful weapons. Now, countries are concentrating their efforts on developing smaller, smarter weapons.

Trends in technology In the twentieth century, the trend toward more and more powerful weapons and longer-range weapons led to the most powerful and longest-range weapons ever created—intercontinental nuclear missiles. In the twenty-first century, military technology is trying to do more with less. Military technology is also more accurate than ever. Greater accuracy means that fewer weapons can be used, causing fewer casualties.

The information war We live in the information age. Information has never been more important in warfare, too. The challenge for the future is to develop ways of bringing all the data, pictures, maps, and other information together, analyzing it quickly, and presenting it to troops on the ground in a way that they can take in fast and use before it is out-of-date. Future soldiers may have important information projected onto the inside of their helmet visors.

Modern military operations require the collection and analysis of enormous amounts of information. This is often managed from at least one control room. This room is the System Control Room for the Iraq war, which began in 2003, at Camp Doha in Qatar.

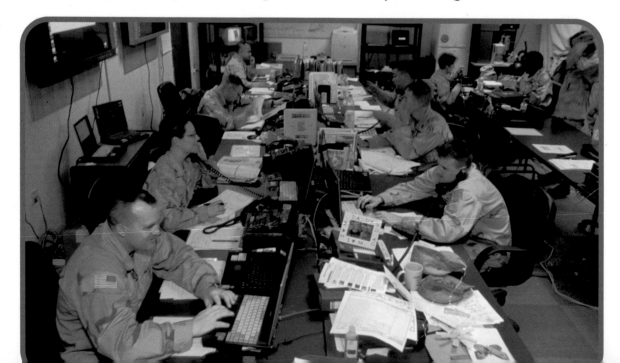

Robots The number of military robots is set to increase rapidly. The U.S. is aiming to replace one-third of its armed vehicles and weaponry with robots by 2015.

How does military technology affect us? We all make use of military technology in one way or another. The Internet was developed as a way of protecting computer systems from a military attack. The technology used for weather forecasts can trace its history back to photoreconnaissance in WWI and WWII. The rockets that launch satellites and spacecraft were developed from rocket-powered weapons built in the 1940s. GPS satellite navigation used by drivers was developed for military use.

Fighting terrorism The 9/11 attacks on the U.S. in 2001 showed that terrorist organizations can bypass the most high-tech military weapons and forces to attack cities. Much of the military technology developed up to now is useless against terrorist attack. Future military technology will have to find new ways of fighting terrorism. However, many of these techniques will violate the privacy of millions of people, who will have to decide how much privacy they are prepared to give up for increased security.

WHAT'S NEXT?

Information technology is the weapon that will be used against terrorists. Facial recognition systems will identify known terrorists on city streets. Computerized cameras will spot unusual body language that may reveal a terrorist. Automatic analysis of electronic communication will give early warning of attacks being planned. Electronic sniffers will detect explosives and other dangerous chemicals.

New security systems, such as biometric fingerprint scanning, are already being introduced at airports around the world.

glossary

acoustic To do with sound. An acoustic weapon is a weapon that uses sound.

antennas The parts of radio systems that send out or receive radio signals.

artificial intelligence The development of computers which can reason in a similar way to the human brain.

autonomous Independent. An autonomous aircraft flies under its own control without a pilot.

classified Information that should only be seen by certain authorized personnel.

Cold War The period of hostility between democratic and communist countries after World War II.

exoskeleton Literally, an "external skeleton." A powered robot-like suit or frame that enables a soldier to carry a heavier load or move faster.

gamma ray High-energy electromagnetic radiation.

gunship A helicopter or airplane heavily armed with guns.

hull The part of a ship that sits in the water.

hypersonic Faster than Mach 5 (five times the speed of sound).

infrared Invisible lightwaves whose wavelength is longer than light but shorter than radio waves.

intercontinental missile A missile that can travel from one continent to the other.

laser A device that produces an intensely powerful beam of light. Laser stands for Light Amplification by Stimulated Emission of Radiation.

microwaves Very short radio waves, 1-30 millimeters long.

payload The passengers, cargo, or bombs carried by an aircraft.

prototype The first full-size, working version of something. Prototypes are built to test vehicles and weapons before they are manufactured in large numbers.

radar A system for detecting and locating aircraft, rockets, ships, and other vehicles and weapons by sending out radio waves and picking up any reflections that bounce back after striking these objects. Radar stands for RAdio Detection And Ranging.

reconnaissance Spying on enemy forces or land. Aircraft and satellites are often used for reconnaissance by flying over an area and photographing it. This is also called photoreconnaissance.

stealth plane A military aircraft designed to be hard to find by radar.

submersible A small underwater vehicle.

supersonic Something that travels faster than the speed of sound.

more information

Books

The World's Greatest Warplanes
by Ian Graham, Raintree Publishers, 2005.

Technology All Around Us: Aircraft
by Kay Woodward and Andrew Woodward,
Smart Apple Media, 2005.

Web Sites

How Military Robots Work
http://science.howstuffworks.com/
military-robot.htm
Read this article to meet some of the
military's latest robot soldiers, find out what
sorts of jobs they can do and get a glimpse
of what the future holds for military robots.

Military Channel: Abrams Tank
http://military.discovery.com/convergence/
abrams/abrams.html
See photos of the Abrams tank in action and
view a clickable picture of the tank that
explains each part.

Smithsonian: How does GPS work?
www.nasm.si.edu/gps/work.html
Learn how GPS devices connect to satellites
and calculate their position.

Independence Class Littoral Combat Ship
http://www.defense-update.com/products/l/
lcs-independence.htm
Read about the Littoral Combat Ship, the
U.S. Navy's new trimaran warship.

Places to Visit

National Air and Space Museum
Washington, D.C.
The world's largest collection of historic air
and spacecraft
http://www.nasm.si.edu/museum/

Air Force Museum
Dayton, Ohio
The world's largest military
aviation museum
www.nationalmuseum.af.mil

Strategic Air and Space Museum
Bellevue, Nebraska
Museum preserving the history of the
Strategic Air Command
http://www.strategicairandspace.com/

U.S. Navy Submarine Force Museum
Groton, Connecticut
Home of the *USS Nautilus*, the first nuclear-
powered submarine
http://www.ussnautilus.org

Naval Undersea Museum
Silverdale, Washington
A large collection of artifacts related to
naval undersea history, science, and
operations
https://www.keyportmuseum.cnrnw.navy.mil

index

Numbers in *italic* refer to illustrations.